Lines, Bars and Circles

How William Playfair
Invented Graphs

To troublemakers everywhere — H.B.
For Patrice, who loves statistics and charts! — M-È.T.

Acknowledgments

Thank you to the Ontario Arts Council for its support
in the creation of this project. Thanks also to Professor Ian Spence,
University of Toronto. His expertise and generous input on the life
and works of William Playfair made this book significantly better
than it otherwise would be.

Kids Can Press gratefully acknowledges the financial
support of the Government of Ontario, through the
Ontario Media Development Corporation; the Ontario
Arts Council; the Canada Council for the Arts; and
the Government of Canada, through the CBF, for our
publishing activity.

Published in Canada and the U.S. by Kids Can Press Ltd.
25 Dockside Drive, Toronto, ON M5A 0B5

Kids Can Press is a Corus Entertainment Inc. company

www.kidscanpress.com

The artwork in this book was rendered digitally in
Photoshop.

Edited by Stacey Roderick
Designed by Julia Naimska

Printed and bound in Shenzhen, China, in 10/2016
through Asia Pacific Offset

CM 17 0 9 8 7 6 5 4 3 2 1

**Library and Archives Canada Cataloguing in
Publication**

Becker, Helaine, 1961–, author
    Lines, bars and circles : how William Playfair
invented graphs / written by Helaine Becker ; illustrated
by Marie-Ève Tremblay.

ISBN 978-1-77138-570-1 (hardback)

    1. Playfair, William, 1759–1823 — Juvenile literature.
2. Mathematical statistics — Graphic methods —
History — Juvenile literature. 3. Graphic methods —
History — Juvenile literature. 4. Mathematical statistics
— Graphic methods — Juvenile literature. 5. Graphic
methods — Juvenile literature. 6. Mathematics —
Graphic methods — Juvenile literature. 7. Mathematics
— Charts, diagrams, etc. — Juvenile literature.
I. Tremblay, Marie-Ève, 1978 July 19–, illustrator II.
Title.

QA276.13.B43 2017   j001.4'226   C2016-902244-7

Lines, Bars and Circles

How William Playfair Invented Graphs

Written by **Helaine Becker**

Illustrated by **Marie-Ève Tremblay**

Kids Can Press

William Playfair was a dreamer. He saw the world differently from other people.

Will was also a joker who saw humor where others didn't. He could be very annoying, especially to his sisters and brothers.

When Will was twelve years old, his father died. Soon after, Will's oldest brother, John, moved back to the family's home near Dundee, Scotland, and took over Will's education.

The brothers were nothing alike. John was a scientist and mathematician. He saw the world in numbers and formulas.

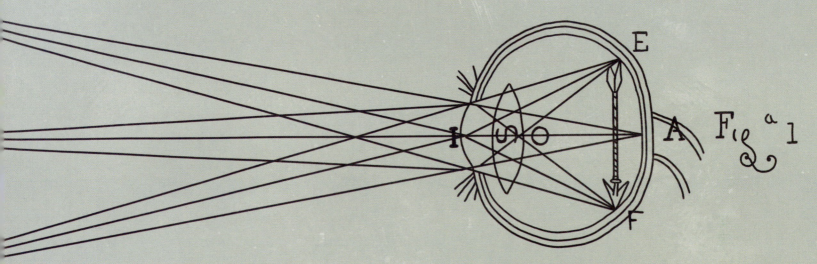

With John in charge, Will had to shape up. No more playing practical jokes or drawing fanciful pictures. Will would have to learn how to think — and behave — more like a scientist. More like John.

Naturally, Will thought *John* was very annoying.

The Scientific Method

During the 1700s in Scotland, many people, including William's brother John, followed a new and important way of thinking called the Scientific Method. Using the Scientific Method, scientists start with a hypothesis — a possible reason for why something happens. Then they test that hypothesis with an experiment. This process is still used today and has helped us understand everything from the tiniest microbes to the most distant stars.

Nevertheless, John was a good teacher.
He taught Will how to measure temperature on
a thermometer and to correctly and clearly record
the information each day in tables and charts.

Will found himself becoming an excellent mathematician. And a *bit* more like John.

But Will didn't — *couldn't* — stop dreaming.
Nor could he stop seeing the world in his own way.

That made him restless. And that made him
more annoying than ever to John!

So when Will was fourteen, he left home
and got a job working for an inventor named
Andrew Meikle.

Meikle was a dreamer, too.

Meikle designed and built the machines used in grain mills. He taught Will how to draw plans for and make many different kinds of machines.

Now Will could picture a magnificent future for himself. He would have untold

riches!

fame!

glory!

After a few years, though, Meikle's workshop felt too small to hold all Will's grand dreams.

So Will got a new job. He became an assistant to James Watt, a famous inventor and draftsman who Will worshipped for his cleverness and creativity. Will's days were spent problem solving and drawing detailed plans for machinery.

He was in the thick of the action now! In Watt's workshop, he met dozens of famous scientists and inventors.

Inspired, he started thinking of inventions of his own. In fact, Will was so busy picturing new ideas, he didn't pay enough attention to his work. He wound up annoying his boss, who called Will a blunderer. Watt complained that Will took too many shortcuts and made too many mistakes.

The Industrial Revolution

The Industrial Revolution was a period in history (from around 1760 to 1840) when new ways of manufacturing were being invented. James Watt was one of its key players — his improvement to the steam engine allowed tasks that had always been done by hand to be done by machine. Because of the steam engine, as well as many other inventions, industries like textiles and metalworking grew quickly, bringing wealth to the people and nations that owned them. New kinds of transportation, such as the steamboat and the steam-powered locomotive, meant goods and people traveled farther and more cheaply than ever before. The Industrial Revolution changed the way people lived and worked forever.

Eventually, Will decided to strike out on his own.

While working for Watt, Will had invented a machine that made beautiful objects out of silver, so he decided to open a shop. In it, he sold all sorts of splendid silver goods: fancy buckles, superior horseshoes, special spoons …

FANCY

SUPERIOR

SPECIAL

VERY GOOD PRICES!

Nevertheless, the shop failed. It seemed Will was better at envisioning new ideas than running a business.

Losing his business was disappointing, but it still didn't stop Will from picturing himself coming out on top!

To get there, he would try writing articles, editing newspapers, making cannon parts for the British army and even running a bank. But every venture failed. Worse, his schemes often got him into trouble. He even came close to being thrown in jail!

If only people could see things as he did. If they could, he was sure he wouldn't be flat broke …

he wouldn't be in trouble with the law …

he'd finally have untold

riches!

fame!

glory!

When he wasn't dreaming up new business schemes, Will wrote books. It earned him a bit of money, and it allowed him to write about things he was passionate about: history, politics and economics.

For one of his books, Will didn't have all the information he needed to complete a chart. To solve this problem, he drew two numbered lines: one running up and down that represented quantities and one running along the bottom that represented time. Next, he plotted dots in the chart to represent the data he did have. Then he connected the dots.

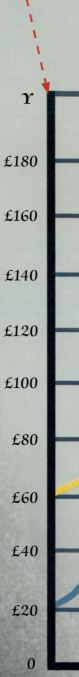

The y-axis is read from the bottom up.

Y

£180

£160

£140

£120

£100

£80

£60

£40

£20

0

1700

With these steps, he had turned numbers and time into a picture. He had created the line graph.

Imports and Exports

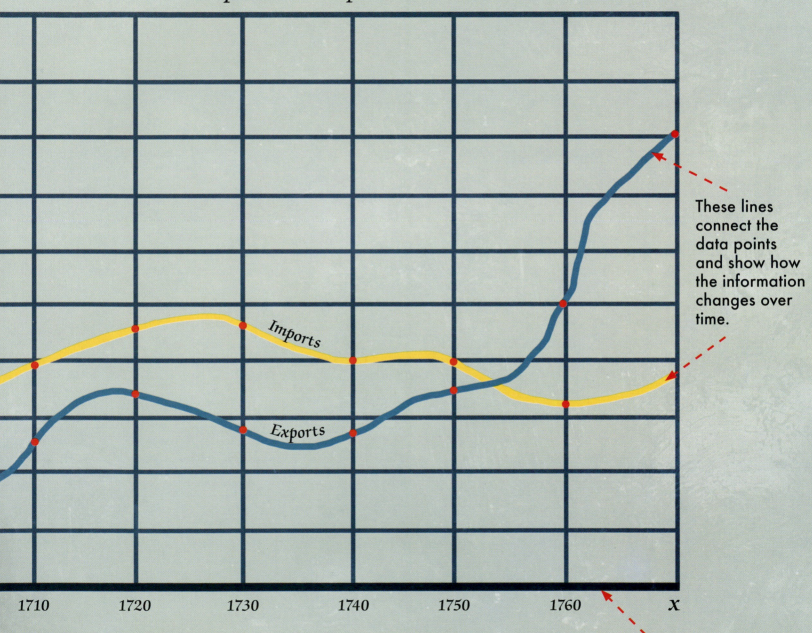

These lines connect the data points and show how the information changes over time.

1710   1720   1730   1740   1750   1760   *x*

The x-axis is read from left to right.

The line graph had turned out to be more than just a clever way of showing information. It made the information clearer and easier to remember, too.

When he wanted to include a second chart that had even fewer details, he came up with another good idea: he grouped the information into chunks.

Now Will had created the bar graph!

He knew he was onto something with his new charts.

Y

400

350

300

250

200

Ten Thousands in Pounds

150

100

0

America

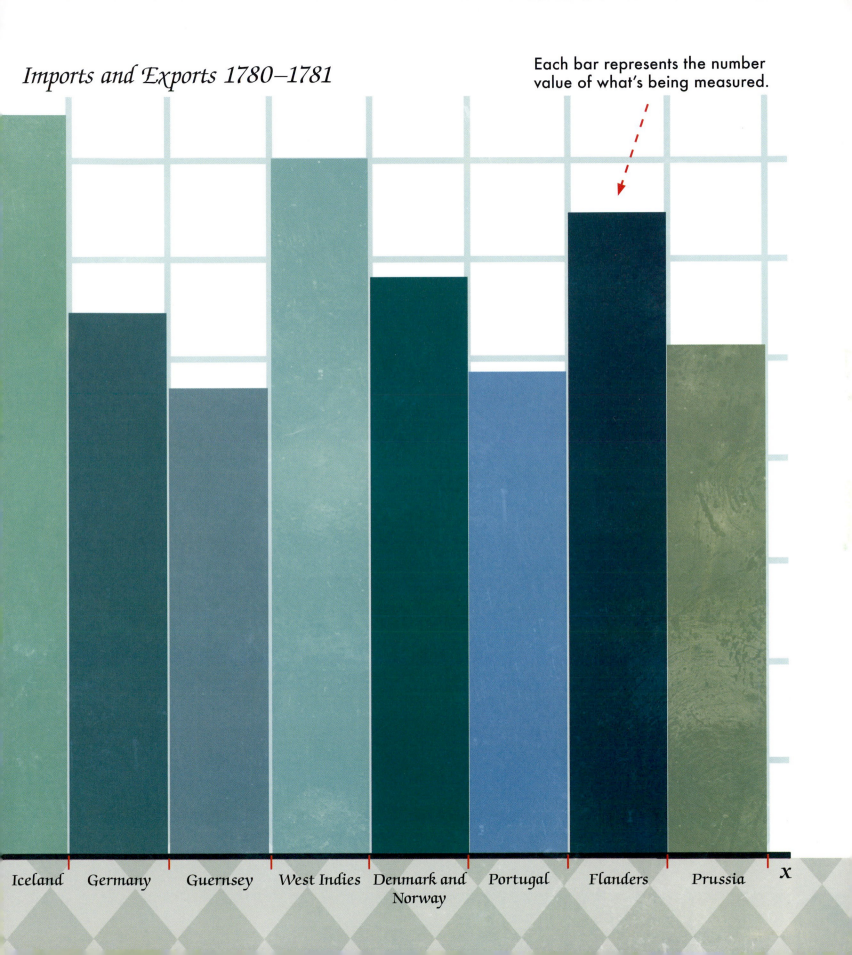

Imports and Exports 1780–1781

Each bar represents the number value of what's being measured.

Iceland   Germany   Guernsey   West Indies   Denmark and Norway   Portugal   Flanders   Prussia   **x**

King Louis XVI of France also liked Will's graphs. He agreed that they were easy to understand. In fact, the king liked them so much that he rewarded Will with a royal permit.

The permit allowed Will to build a steam-powered rolling mill that would manufacture all kinds of objects out of steel. If it was successful, he'd make plenty of money.

But alas, before the mill got rolling, the king was overthrown. Will had to run for his life!

The French Revolution

In 1789, the people of France were very angry with their king and queen, King Louis XVI and Queen Marie Antoinette. They believed the royal couple and the rest of the nobility lived in luxury while everyone else suffered and starved. Inspired by the American Revolution, the French citizens overthrew and executed their king and queen. During the Revolution, many who supported the royal family were executed, too.

Once he arrived safely in England, Will kept writing … and dreaming up new ways of showing numbers in pictures.

Another time, he divided a circle into slices to show the relationship of its parts to the whole.

This was the first pie chart!

Types of Grain Planted, by Acre

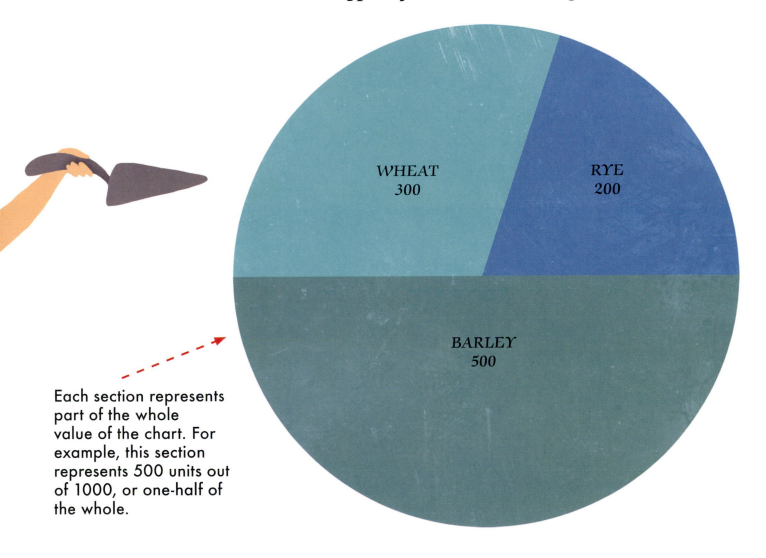

WHEAT
300

RYE
200

BARLEY
500

Each section represents part of the whole value of the chart. For example, this section represents 500 units out of 1000, or one-half of the whole.

With all his charts, Will believed he had invented valuable tools for sharing hard-to-understand information. What a future he could see for himself now! His glorious destiny *must* be assured at last.

But it was not to be. At least, not in his lifetime.

The scientists of his day turned up their noses at Will's graphs. They saw them as nothing but a distraction. Numbers showed serious work, colorful illustrations did not.

They also thought of Will as a ne'er-do-well with a long string of business failures behind him. They couldn't — *wouldn't* — believe someone like that could have invented anything truly valuable.

Maybe they would have taken him seriously if he'd been more like his brother John.

Yet if William Playfair had been like his brother, he might not have invented his charts. It's true Will was, at times, a scoundrel and a schemer. But he was also an independent thinker who was able to see things differently from those around him.

It took almost a hundred years, but eventually the graphs caught on. Now, line graphs, bar graphs and pie charts are used around the world to explain all kinds of information. Just as Will had pictured.

More About William and His Charts

A true jack-of-all-trades, William Playfair (1759–1823) was an engineer, a silversmith, an economist, a writer, an inventor and an entrepreneur. Most importantly, though, he almost single-handedly invented the three most widely used styles of infographics: the modern line graph, bar graph and pie chart.

Why, then, doesn't everyone know his name?

Part of the reason might be because he lived in a time when a person's reputation meant everything. And unfortunately for William, his was not good. At all. His big dreams and ambition often got the better of him. He tended to brag outrageously and often broke promises. He got into arguments and stole money from investors. He was even convicted of fraud! William's behavior raised eyebrows — and lowered expectations — of the people around him. If he hadn't been such a scoundrel, his ideas might not have been overlooked for so long.

Another likely reason his line graph, bar graph and pie chart weren't immediately embraced was that they challenged the conventions of the time. In his day, numbers were all that counted in science. Pictures were considered "works of imagination." For scientists and mathematicians to see how illustrations could also be useful tools meant they had to be able to think "outside the box." But as a dreamer who seemed to see the world differently from those around him, William was just the one to be able to do this.

William's Early Life

William came of age during the Scottish Enlightenment. This was a golden age in Scotland, prompted by the earlier Scientific Revolution, when the newly discovered Scientific Method was applied to all fields of inquiry, from the nature of electricity to the workings of the human body. As a result, Scotland experienced an economic boom, as well as a flourishing art and literary scene.

Not much is known about William's early home life or the events surrounding his father's death when William was just twelve. What we do know is that when William's older brother, John, a famous mathematician, returned home to take over William's education, John trained his younger brother rigorously in science and mathematics. William wrote that John had "made me keep a register of a thermometer, expressing the variations by lines on a divided scale. He taught me to know, that, whatever can be expressed in numbers, may be represented by lines."

John also taught William how to read and understand logic diagrams, maps and even a time line created by Joseph Priestley (the theologian and chemist credited with discovering oxygen). It seems likely that having such a deep understanding of these graphic-oriented tools served as a springboard for William's own innovations.

William and His "Charts"

William's first important breakthrough — the statistical line graph — appeared in his 1786 book *The Commercial and Political Atlas*. By writing the book, William had hoped to make a name — and some money — for himself as a scholar in the fields of history and economics. The graphs (which William called "charts," a name inspired by nautical charts and maps) had all of the key elements of a modern line graph: labeled horizontal and vertical axes; marks indicating units of time; color and shading to highlight different elements; and a title and a caption explaining the source of the data. No earlier chart used all of these features. Nor had any tried to do what William's chart did, which was show precise numerical data and the changes to that data over time using an illustration.

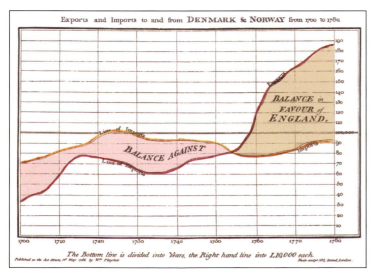

William's innovative line graph from **The Commercial and Political Atlas,** *1786*

William's bar graph, also the first of its kind, appeared in *The Commercial and Political Atlas* as well. It was based on Joseph Priestley's *A Chart of Biography* (1765), which had also used lines to represent longer or shorter periods of time and larger or smaller quantities. When William didn't have enough data to plot onto a line for one of the line graphs he had planned, he chunked the data that he did have into groups. This style of displaying data wound up showing larger patterns in the data that might not have been noticed when plotted in a line graph.

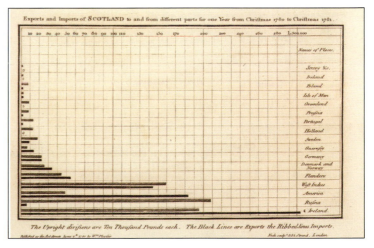

William's bar graph from **The Commercial and Political Atlas,** *1786*

William's final invention, the pie chart (or, as it is called in France, "the Camembert," after the round cheese), appeared in his 1801 book *Statistical Breviary*. These were the first circular charts to be divided into fractional parts or sections that accurately represented their share of the whole. He also used different colors to differentiate each part.

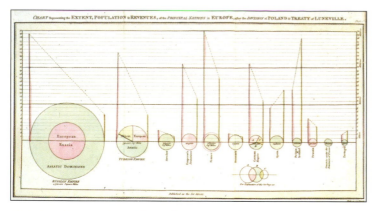

William's pie chart from **Statistical Breviary, 1801**

William felt sure that his new charts were special and that they would help people understand information faster and more easily than number-filled tables. But he also knew he would have a difficult time convincing others of their usefulness, so he included an explanation in *The Commercial and Political Atlas* for "those who do not, at first sight, understand the manner of inspecting the charts." In it, he promised that if readers spent just a few minutes looking at the pictures, all their doubts "would entirely vanish, and as much information may be obtained in five minutes as would require whole days to imprint on the memory, in a lasting manner, by a table of figures."

The king of France, who had been given a copy of the book by a British lord, agreed with William, who later wrote, "[the king] at once understood the charts and was highly pleased. He said they spoke all languages and were very clear and easily understood."

In appreciation, King Louis XVI approved a rarely offered permit for William to build a steam-powered mill in France. The deal of a lifetime for William, this was a chance to make a lot of money and win him the prestige he craved.

William's Later Life

William's financial fortune was not to change, however. The mill never began production, in part because William got involved in a questionable scheme and was accused of stealing. He fled France just before the 1793 Reign of Terror, a period of time during the French Revolution when anyone associated with the king could be rounded up and murdered.

This wouldn't be the only time in his life that William was involved in shady dealings. His ego often led him to attempt ventures that were beyond his capabilities. He was even convicted of two crimes! (Once for insulting and making false statements about a French count and another time for a bad business deal.) And toward the end of his life, when he was desperate for money, he even tried to blackmail one of the richest men in England. (Luckily for William, this wasn't discovered until after his death.)

Despite his many talents and oversized ambition, William did not achieve the fame or fortune he so badly wanted. His revolutionary graphic devices were ignored or scorned by his contemporaries. When he died in 1823 in England, it seemed likely that his ideas would die with him.

But, of course, we know they didn't. It took more than a hundred years, but eventually William's picture charts were rediscovered and put to use. Today, infographics are used everywhere — in magazines, in newspapers, on TV weather forecasts, in science papers and government documents, and in kindergarten classrooms and university lecture halls.